SUDDEN GRAVITY

A TALE OF THE PANOPTICON

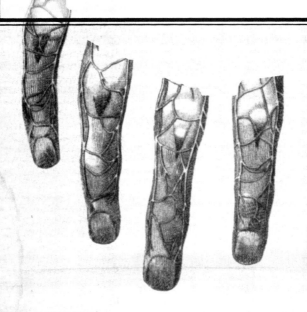

For Jen

Special thanks to those who allowed their
physical visages to be so corrupted for the
sake of this book you now hold: Alex Gargilis,
Arrow Kleeman, Denise Fasanello Jen Smith,
Bill Riley, Roxanne Wolanczynck, Andrew
Kennedy, Mike Ferarra, Christian Hawkins,
Rebeckah Brooks, John Patterson, Travis
and Milah Libbon

Bloated and untreatable thanks to Allen Spiegel
and especially to Shawna Gore for her enthusiasm,
editorial prowess, squirrels, and friendship.

Designed by Greg Ruth
Published by Mike Richardson

Published by Dark Horse Books,
a division of Dark Horse Comics
10956 S.E. Main St.
Milwaukie, OR 97222

www.darkhorse.com

First edition: July 2006
ISBN-10: 1-59307-565-0
ISBN-13: 978-1-59307-565-1

1 3 5 7 9 10 8 6 4 2

PRINTED IN CANADA

"Under the Maud Moon" from The Book of Nightmares by Galway Kinnell copyright 1971 Houghton/Mifflin
A Morning's Work: Photographs from the Burns Archive & Collection 1843-1939. Stanley Burns 1998 Twin Palms Press

SUDDEN GRAVITY
A TALE OF THE PANOPTICON

story and art
by
GREG RUTH

edited by
SHAWNA GORE

Dark Horse Books™

A Note from the Editor

Dear Reader,

　　You are about to embark on an adventure in reading
that may well be unparalleled in your previous experiences.
Sudden Gravity: A Tale of the Panopticon could handily be
filed under the genre label of "mystery," though the presence
of some supernatural elements have led this publisher to
categorize it under "horror." Fair enough, one could argue.

　　However, readers with an acute sense for the absurd
might find themselves questioning, "Is this humor I detect?"
Humor is also present, we assure you, however subtle it may
seem.

　　Categorizing aside, at the heart of this story is a
conspiracy theory that has overtaken an antiquated mental
institution, acted out by a cast of characters who will seem
extremely real to you, despite their own paper-locked
existences. Drawn together by the civic need to care for and
examine those society labels as everything from "mentally
challenged" to "criminally insane," these characters, the hospital's
staff and patients alike, are each a study of human error. Some
of this error is specific to the individual. Most of it is specifc to
humanity itself.

　　Magniloquent language aside, what we're really talking
about is the perception of reality, how that can bend toward
sanity or insanity, and the preposterous lengths people will
embark upon to conceal what frightens us. Humanity's history
is a sordid one, and this book serves as a text to that point.
And while we're on the topic of sanity, we would like to question
that of the author and artist of this book, who chose to document
these events not as most artists in this medium would, with fine
tools such as brush and ink, but with the pedestrian tool known
as a BIC brand ball-point pen. Should any rooms at the
Panopticon become available in the near future, we are
recommending Mr. Ruth be invited over for at least a short
stay.

Sincerely,

The Editor

FIVE DAYS LEFT

It's beginning again.

i try to wake myself up, but I can't.

it's the same dream every night since the **fire**.

it's a **voice** in my head— but not **words**. it's **pictures**...

and...

and there's someone **else** there.

. the **boy** in room 13.

7

10

GUESS THAT'S WHAT I *GET* FOR WATCHIN' THE NEWS, HUH?

AND DON'T YOU *FORGET* IT EITHER.

YOU THINK PEOPLE LIKE THE COMMISONER BACK THERE WANT YOU TO KNOW WHAT'S *REALLY* GOING ON?

BENTHAM HOSPITAL EXIT ¼ MILE

THINK IF *YOU* KILLED YOUR FAMILY AND BURNED DOWN YOUR HOUSE YOU'D GET A RIDE TO A *COZY* HOSPITAL ROOM INSTEAD OF THE FRIGGIN' *CHAIR?*

YOU DON'T WANNA GET ME *STARTED* HERE, DARRYL.

YOU MEAN YOU AIN'T *ALREADY* STARTED YET?

ASK ME, OL' ALICE HERE, PLAYED HER CARDS PRETTY SWEETLY.

LOTTA FOLKS BEEN LOSING THEIR HOMES TO THE CITY *BULLDOZERS,* AND SHE'S BEEN IN THE FRIGGIN' CAPTAIN'S CHAIR OF IT *ALL,* MAN.

AND FOR *WHAT?* WHAT THEY GOTTA BUILD IN THEIR PLACE THAT PEOPLE NEED MORE THAN THEIR *HOMES,* HUH?

"EXPANSION OF INFRASTRUCTURE" MY *ASS.*

I MEAN, THIS GODDAMNED *HOSPITAL* ALREADY BLOCKS OUT HALF THE *SUN,* MAN.

WE REALLY NEED MORE OF *THIS?*

... AND TO EVACUATE THE *WHOLE* BUILDING!

GENARO'S ALSO SUSPENDING AUGET'S TRANSFER *AGAIN.*

RUMOR HAS IT HE'S BEEN ASSIGNED THE *ALICE SPARK* CASE.

WOW, HE'S GOING TO BE *PISSED.*

I WONDER *WHO* GETS TO TELL ...

... HIM

I THINK *YOU* JUST DID, STRAUSS.

WAY TO *GO,* SLICK.

NEVER MAKE FUN OF A *PATHOLOGIST,* BARRY.

... IF YOU *DON'T* GET BACK IN LINE I'M GOING TO DO SOMETHING *YOU'LL* REGRET LATER.

LOOK, PAL ...

JUSTICE!

JUSTICE FOR THE VICTIMS!

PAMELA, *WHAT* THE HELL IS GOING *ON* OUT HERE?

WHO *ARE* ALL THESE PEOPLE?

OH, IT'S JUST YOUR NEW PATIENT'S *FAN* CLUB.

FRY ALICE SPARK!!

JUSTICE!

FRY ALICE SPARK!!

THE *NEXT* TIME YOU PEOPLE DECIDE TO PLAY ROCK STAR DOCTOR TO THE RICH AND NOTORIOUS, I'D *APPRECIATE* A LITTLE HEADS UP.

I'M NOT EVEN SUPPOSED TO BE HERE TODAY, YOU KNOW? I'M *SUPPOSED* TO BE AT HOME WITH MY SOAPS.

BUT YOU DON'T GIVE A *RAT'S ASS* DO YOU?

I'M A *RECEPTIONIST*, NOT A GODDAMNED *ZOOKEEPER*.

YOU WANT *CROWD CONTROL*, CALL THE DAMN COPS.

I ONLY ASKED IF--

OH *SURE*, THAT'S HOW IT *ALWAYS* STARTS.

NEXT YOU'LL BE ASKING--

LET GO OF MY COAT THIS *INSTANT* YOU SCALAWAG, OR I SHALL THRASH YOU SENSELESS!

GREAT. HERE COMES *ANOTHER* ONE.

DON'T EVEN *SAY* IT, BARNES. I'M IN *NO* MOOD.

MUST I PICK UP THE BLASTED PHONE *MYSELF?*

OH, I'M *SORRY* PAMELA, I THOUGHT YOU *WORKED* HERE. HAVE YOU NOT CALLED THE BLOODY COPS?

DAVID, WHAT'S THIS ABOUT MY *TRANSFER?* I HEARD THAT *GENARO* HAS BLOCKED IT AGAIN! HOW CAN I *POSSIBLY*--

IT WASN'T *GENARO'S* IDEA HENRY, IT WAS *MINE.*

SORRY. YOU CAN'T LEAVE NOW. SOMETHING *DREADFUL* IS AFOOT.

YOU? BUT...

... YOU *INITIATED* THE TRANSFER!

THIS ASSIGNMENT WAS *SUPPOSED* TO BE ONLY *TEMPORARY.*

IT'S BEEN OVER A *YEAR*, ALREADY!

YES, I *KNOW.* BUT YOU MUST UNDERSTAND, I HAD NO *CHOICE.*

I'M AFRAID WE CAN'T DISCUSS THIS HERE.

WHY NOT? *PAMELA* SEEMS TO KNOW MORE ABOUT THIS THAN *I* DO!

BECAUSE *SHE IS HERE* NOW.

14

15

IT'S OPEN.

HENRY. I SUPPOSE AN APOLOGY IS IN ORDER.

I'D MUCH RATHER HAVE MY *TRANSFER*, LOUIS.

HEARING ABOUT IT FROM HALLWAY GOSSIP JUST BEFORE MEETING MY NEW PATIENT WAS A NICE TOUCH, I MIGHT ADD.

PULL UP A CHAIR AND LET ME TELL YOU A LITTLE STORY.

LAST WEEK, THE MAYOR'S OFFICE CONTACTED US TO "EVALUATE" MS. SPARK'S CONDITION.

IN ORDER TO DETERMINE IF SHE'S *FIT* TO STAND TRIAL.

HMPH. THAT'S A BIT *OUT* OF THEIR AREA.

YES IT *IS*.

I'VE JUST HUNG UP WITH WITH THE ATTORNEY GENERAL. HE WAS VERY *UPSET*.

UPSET, *WHY*?

APPARENTLY WE'VE TAKEN TOO LONG TO FIND HER COMPETENT.

WAIT. I DON'T GET IT. SHE'S ONLY *JUST* NOW ARRIVED. I JUST MET HER WITH DAVID IN THE MAIN HALL.

YES I *KNOW*.

SOUNDS LIKE A SET-UP DOESN'T IT? AND A *CLUMSY* ONE AT THAT.

BUT IF IT'S A ...

PRETTY *NEAT*, HUH?

ROMULUS AND RAYMOND, TWO OF DR. BARNES' PATIENTS, PAINTED THAT FOR ME.

LIKE IT?

NOT REALLY, NO.

IT THINK IT'S CREEPY AND A LITTLE *DISTURBING*.

HEH.

YOU KNOW THEY ASKED FOR *YOU* SPECIFICALLY TO PERFORM THE SO-CALLED *EVALUATION* ON MS. SPARK.

ME? *WHY?*

HMM ... I HOPED *YOU* MIGHT KNOW. LET'S GIVE THEM WHAT THEY WANT AND *SEE* WHERE IT ALL GOES.

BUT FIRST I WANT YOU OVER AT ST. VINCENT'S TO LOOK INTO MR. SPARK'S REMAINS. BE *DISCREET.* YOU CAN SAY YOU'RE JUST VISITING YOUR OLD RESIDENCY.

AND THERE'S ONE MORE THING. THEY'RE SENDING SOMEONE OUT TO PICK HER UP.

YOU'RE *JOKING!* WHEN?

IMMEDIATELY, I WOULD ASSUME. YOU'LL HAVE TO GET *STRAIGHT* TO WORK WITH HER--AS SOON AS YOU GET BACK FROM ST. VINCENT'S.

I WANT A REPORT EVERY TWO HOURS.

NOW GO FIND WHAT THEY *DON'T* WANT US TO LOOK FOR, HENRY.

HENRY, OVER *HERE*.

HELRO DOCTRURH AUTHAY!

ITH ITH A BEURTHIFUL THAY?

HAH!

IT IS NOW THAT I'VE SEEN, *YOU*, MARGARET.

SUSAN. NICE *MOHAIR*. WHAT HAPPENED TO YOUR COAT?

AHH ... MARGARET HAD A SPELL OF *NAUSEA* EARLY TODAY.

I'VE PUKEDTH *FREE* THIMES ALREADTHY!

I THINK YOU'VE JUST BROKEN BARRY WINSLOW'S OLD *RECORD*, MARGARET!

YAY! HAH!

ECHM ... *SORRY* ABOUT THAT THING IN THE HALL EARLIER.

YOU KNOW, ABOUT YOUR *TRANSFER* AND ALL.

YEAH, WELL ... WATER UNDER THE BRIDGE.

BARRY AND STRAUSS ARE IN HIDING, FEARING *REVENGE*.

HOW *OLD* ARE THEY AGAIN?

WHERE ARE YOU HEADED NOW?

ST. VINCENT'S FOR A LITTLE VISIT WITH MR. SPARK'S *HUSBAND*.

URP... I FINK I'M GONNA BREAKTH A RECORDTH AGAIN, SUTHAN ...

LET'S GO, SWEETIE.

URRP.

GOING TO BE *WEIRD* BEING AT ST. VINNIE'S AGAIN AFTER WHAT *HAPPENED*, HENRY.

GOOD *LUCK* OUT THERE.

YEAH ...

I'M AFRAID SO.

IT'S *GLOSSOLALIA*. HOLY SPEECH. IT'S ENGLISH SPOKEN *BACKWARDS*.

WELL, WHAT DOES IT *MEAN*?

JULIUS WAS RAISED IN A *PENTECOSTAL* CULT IN PLANO, TEXAS.

THE CULT WAS *OBSESSED* WITH CHILDREN. THEY BELIEVED HUMANITY'S TIME WAS AT AN *END*, AND IT WOULD SOON GIVE BIRTH TO A *HOLY RACE* THAT WOULD CLEANSE THE EARTH OF *SIN*.

LOVELY.

JULIUS IS NAMED FOR GAIUS JULIUS CAESAR, AND WAS ALSO EXPECTED TO BIRTH A NEW EMPIRE.

GLOSSOLALIA WAS TO BE THE TONGUE OF THIS NEW ERA.

I'M ONLY FAMILIAR WITH ONE OF THE WORDS YOU'VE JUST NOW READ TO ME...

"EQUINOX".

IT'S *CREEPY* THE WAY HE'S JUST *SITTING* THERE.

IT'S LIKE HE'S JUST *WAITING* FOR SOMETHING, DAVID.

OH, BUT THAT'S *EXACTLY* WHAT HE'S DOING, EMIL.

CHECK YOUR CALENDAR. THE EQUINOX IS IN *FIVE* DAYS.

I WAIT OUTSIDE ST. VINCENT'S FOR ALMOST AN HOUR BEFORE *FINALLY* GOING IN.

WEIRD DOESN'T *BEGIN* TO DESCRIBE WHAT IT'S LIKE TO BE BACK HERE AFTER LAST YEAR.

I'VE BEEN SO *EAGER* TO TRANSFER BACK HERE, AND YET, RIGHT NOW, I CAN'T THINK OF SINGLE REASON *WHY*.

BUT *HERE* I AM, DRAWN BACK ONCE *AGAIN* BY MURDER.

IF THERE IS SOME REASON I HAVE BEEN ASSIGNED THIS CASE, IT IS *NOT* FOR MY TALENTS.

I AM VALUABLE TO SOMEONE IN POWER ONLY FOR MY *WEAKNESS*.

IS IT STILL MURDER IF THEY'RE ALREADY DEAD?

I SUPPOSE THAT'S A QUESTION FOR ANOTHER DAY...

TODAY BELONGS TO ANOTHER CRIME.

THE IRONY SHOULD BE ENOUGH TO MAKE ME SMILE, BUT *WHO* COULD TELL THROUGH THIS MASK?

GOOD MORNING. MR. SPARK.

NICE TO *SEE* YOU AGAIN.

24

25

UH ... YOU KNOW, I'M FROM *TEXAS* MYSELF. ORIGINALLY.

AUSTIN.

DID YOU KNOW AUSTIN HAS THE *LARGEST* POPULATION OF IN-CITY *BATS* IN THE WORLD?

YOU SEE, THEY NEST UNDER THIS OVERPASS...

... AT DUSK THEY JUST COME *FLYING* OUT OF THERE ALL AT *ONCE.*

IT'S LIKE A BIG BLACK INKY *SCREAMING* CLOUD SPILLING INTO THE SKY.

... DEATH.

IT WOULD SCARE MY SISTER AND I TO...

I'M *SORRY.* I DIDN'T MEAN... WELL...UH...

"HMPH... AND THEN WHAT HAPPENED?"

WELL, MOSTLY I KEPT TRYING TO TAKE MY *FOOT* OUT OF MY MOUTH TO MAKE ROOM FOR THE *OTHER* ONE.

CHRIST.

SHE MUST THINK I AM A TOTAL *ASS.*

YOU KNOW FULL WELL THAT IS *NOT* YOUR CONCERN.

27

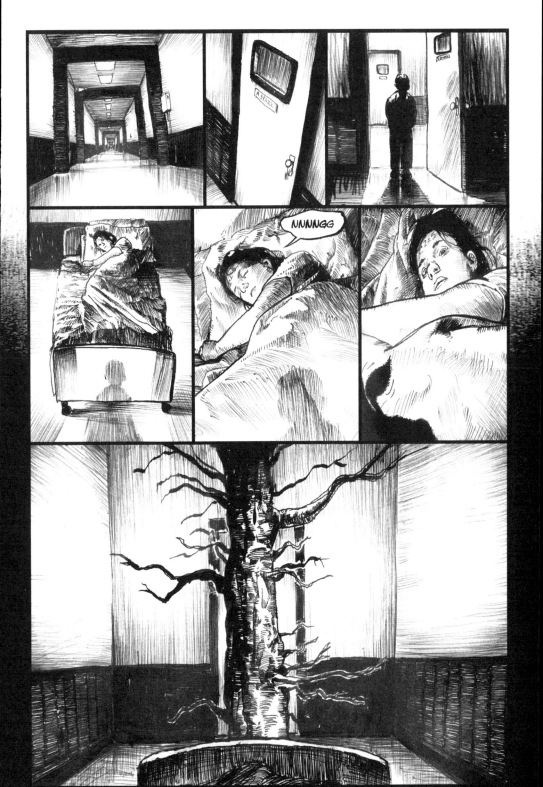

... NO.

DAVID! OKAY, THAT'S IT. I'M CALLING A MEDIC.

NO... NO, I'M *OKAY*. REALLY.

HMPH ... IT'S BEEN SO *LONG* SINCE MY LAST EPISODE... I USED TO GET RATHER *SEVERE* ATTACKS AS A BOY.

I DIDN'T KNOW YOU WERE EPILEPTIC.

WELL, HEH...

IT'S NOT EXACTLY THE *FIRST* THING YOU PUT ON YOUR RESUME YOU KNOW....

FATHER USED TO TELL ME ABOUT DOSTOYEVSKY'S EPILEPSY TO TRY AND MAKE ME FEEL BETTER ...

IMAGINE... TRYING TO CHEER SOMEONE UP WITH DOSTOYEVSKY.

AS *LONG* AS YOU'RE OKAY...

BY THE *WAY*... THAT TRICK WITH THE LEAF-- HOW'D YOU *DO* THAT?

IT WAS *YOU*, WHO SAW THE DISCONTINUITY. I'M *BLIND*, REMEMBER?

I *MUST* SAY THOUGH, YOU HAVE *QUITE* A KNACK FOR FOCUSING YOUR ATTENTION.

YOU MEDITATE?

NO... I ONLY END UP NODDING OFF.

OH, DAMN!

I WAS SUPPOSED TO REPORT TO GENARO ABOUT MY SESSION WITH ALICE SPARK AND HER HUSBAND HOURS AGO.

...BUT HENRY, ISN'T *MR. SPARK* DECEASED?

EXTREMELY SO, YES.

WELL, OFF YOU GO THEN. I'VE GOT FILES TO FONDLE.

FILES? BUT DAVID, I THOUGHT YOU WERE...

IT'S CALLED *BRAILLE*, YOU TWIT!

..... THERE'S SUSAN NOW.

HEY, WHAT'S GOING ON?

WHAT'S WITH ALL THE COPS?

AH...

MAYBE YOU SHOULD TELL HER, DAVID.

IT'S REALLY YOUR AREA, LOUIS.

AH ... BARRY WINSLOW IS UMM...

DEAD.

... WHAT?

AND...

TELL HER ABOUT JULIUS.

HANG ON.

WHAT HAPPENED TO BARRY?

WE HAVE TO WAIT FOR THE AUTOPSY TO BE SURE...

"... BUT IT WAS PAMELA WHO FOUND HIM.

"SHE WAS HEADING DOWN TO THE ARCHIVES THIS MORNING WHEN SHE SAID SOMETHING CAUGHT HER ATTENTION."

TAP
TAP

HELLO?

"PAMELA SAID SHE SAW A LEG POKING OUT FROM AN OPEN CLOSET DOOR.

"SHE RECOGNIZED BARRY'S SHOES, SO SHE CALLED OUT TO HIM."

BARRY?

"SHE THOUGHT HE'D GOTTEN DRUNK AGAIN AND HAD JUST DUCKED INTO THE CLOSET TO SLEEP IT OFF."

"THAT'S WHEN SHE SAW HIM.

"WHEN I GOT THERE, SHE WAS STILL SCREAMING."

"YOU SEE, WHEN SHE WAS TEN SHE FOUND HER FATHER AFTER HE'D HAD A STROKE.

C'MON BARRY, YOU'LL GET CANNED FOR SURE IF LOUIS FINDS YOU LIKE THIS AGAIN...

"HE DIDN'T MOVE EVEN WHEN SHE NUDGED HIM WITH HER SHOE, SO SHE WENT IN A LITTLE FURTHER.

CHRIST.

WHERE IS PAMELA NOW?

I SENT HER HOME.

OKAY. I'LL GO OUT TO SEE HER AFTER I'VE DONE MY ROUNDS.

WHAT'S ALL THIS ABOUT JULIUS, NOW?

ISN'T HE IN A MILLION-YEAR COMA OR SOMETHING?

UMM... APPARENTLY NOT ANY MORE.

LET'S GO BACK TO MY OFFICE WHERE DAVID AND I CAN BRING YOU UP TO SPEED.

HOPEFULLY WHEN STRAUSS AND AUGET FINISH WITH BARRY'S AUTOPSY...

32

"... WE'LL FIND OUT WHAT THE *HELL* IS GOING ON HERE."

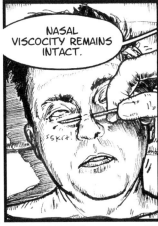

NASAL VISCOCITY REMAINS INTACT.

sskrt!

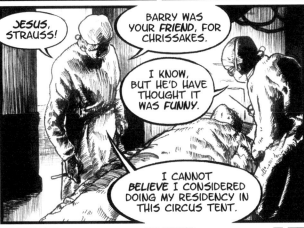

JESUS, STRAUSS!

BARRY WAS YOUR *FRIEND*, FOR CHRISSAKES.

I KNOW, BUT HE'D HAVE THOUGHT IT WAS *FUNNY*.

I CANNOT *BELIEVE* I CONSIDERED DOING MY RESIDENCY IN THIS CIRCUS TENT.

LOOK, MAN ...

...GALLOWS HUMOR IS ABOUT THE ONLY THING KEEPING ME *SANE* RIGHT NOW.

THE EXTEMPORIZED PUMP'S READY.

YOU KNOW, SOMETIMES I GET A LITTLE *DISTURBED* BY WHAT I DO ALL DAY.

WELL, WHY *DO* IT THEN?

I LOVE THE *REALLY* CLEAN AIR THAT'S DOWN HERE.

NUMBER THREE PUMP, PLEASE.

THEY DON'T MAKE A FORMAL-DEHYDE SCENTED DEODORANT YET, DO THEY?

THANKS.

I CAN NEVER TELL IF YOU'RE BEING SERIOUS OR JUST TRYING TO FREAK ME OUT.

SEE *THAT?*

WHAT?

RIGHT *THERE...*

skshlurrpp!

skshhurkk

FOUR DAYS LEFT

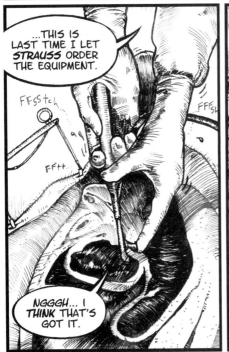

37

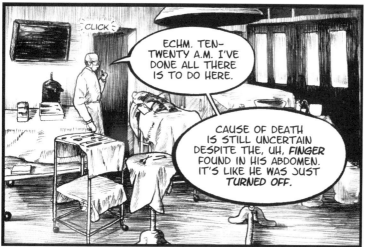

CLICK

ECHM. TEN-TWENTY A.M. I'VE DONE ALL THERE IS TO DO HERE.

CAUSE OF DEATH IS STILL UNCERTAIN DESPITE THE, UH, *FINGER* FOUND IN HIS ABDOMEN. IT'S LIKE HE WAS JUST *TURNED OFF.*

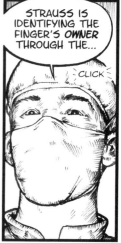

STRAUSS IS IDENTIFYING THE FINGER'S *OWNER* THROUGH THE...

CLICK

CLICK

...THERE'S SOMETHING.

A TATTOO... IT APPEARS TO BE *RECENT.*

STRANGE...

I *KNOW* I'VE SEEN THIS DESIGN BEFORE.

THERE'S A SOUND...

WHAT'S THAT *SOUND?*

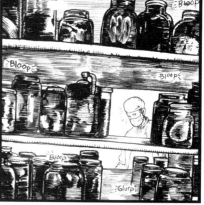

BLOOP

BLOOP

BLOOP

BLOOP

GLUP

BLOOP

GLUB

BLOOP

BLOOP

BLOOP!

BLOOP! BLOOP! LITTHLE THDEAD MAN.

SO WHAT DO THE POLICE SAY?

NOTHING.

IT'S NOT BEEN CONFIRMED THAT IT WAS A MURDER YET.

BLOOP...

REALLY. SO THAT FINGER JUST FELL INTO BARRY'S BODY CAVITY?

WELL.. OBVIOUSLY THAT'S A BIT OF A MYSTERY.

HENRY'S BEEN DOWN THERE ALL NIGHT WITH THE BODY.

ONLY FOUR THOO GO, STHUTHAN!

OH YES, MARGARET! VERY GOOD!

SHE REALLY HAS COME A LONG WAY, DON'T YOU THINK?

YOU'VE DONE A REMARKABLE JOB WITH MARGARET, SUSAN.

HER MOTHER THINKS SO TOO.

SHE SAID YOU CANCELLED HER VISIT LAST WEEK ... AGAIN.

SAID IT WAS THE FIFTH TIME IN A ROW.

SO?

SUSAN... LET'S TAKE A WALK.

AND WHAT IF I DID? I'M HER DOCTOR, LOUIS...

MARGARET?

DR. GENARO AND I WILL BE *RIGHT* OUTSIDE. WILL YOU BE ALL RIGHT?

STHURE!

I'VE GOT MY *THDEAD* MAN!

I KNOW WHAT YOU'RE GOING TO SAY, BUT IT'S *MY* CALL. *JESUS*, HER MOM'S THE REASON SHE'S *IN* HERE, LOUIS!

YOU SHOULD *SEE* HOW MARGARET RECOILS WHEN THAT *WOMAN* VISITS.

HER MOTHER ADMITTED MARGARET *HERSELF*, REMEMBER, SUSAN?

SO WHAT IF SHE DID? SHE *ABUSED*, HER, LOUIS!

SHE IS MARGARET'S *LEGAL* GUARDIAN. I'M JUST TRYING TO *PROTECT* YOU.

OH, *REALLY?*

SHE'S READY TO GO TO THE *BOARD* OVER THIS.

YOU'RE A REMARKABLE CHILD-PSYCHIATRIST, SUSAN, BUT YOU'VE GOTTEN *WAY* TOO CLOSE TO THIS ONE.

BULLSHIT. THIS IS ABOUT US AND YOU *KNOW* IT.

IT'S BEEN *FIVE* YEARS SINCE JACOB DIED, AND YOU STILL WON'T *MOVE ON.*

IF YOU WANT TO KEEP BLAMING OUR BECOMING *INVOLVED* FOR HIS SUICIDE THAT'S *YOUR* AFFAIR...

... BUT YOU *DON'T* GET TO USE ME *OR* MARGARET AS PROXIES FOR WORKING THROUGH YOUR OWN PERSONAL *CRAP.*

IF YOU REMEMBER, YOU WERE THE ONE THAT ENDED IT, LOUIS.

I'VE MOVED ON. DON'T PREACH TO ME ABOUT BEING PROFESSIONAL.

THAT ALL MAY BE TRUE, SUSAN...

ARE YOU THREATENING ME NOW?

...BUT THAT DOESN'T MEAN I'M NOT RIGHT ABOUT THIS. THINK ABOUT WHAT WILL HAPPEN TO MARGARET IF YOU'RE SUSPENDED.

SUSAN, THE OPERATIVE WORD HERE IS MOTHER.

AS HER MOTHER, SHE HAS THE RIGHT TO SEE MARGARET. AS HER ATTENDING, YOU WILL OBLIGE HER.

DON'T MISTAKE MY PATIENCE FOR TOLERANCE, ON THIS ONE.

I AM NOT ASKING YOU TO DO THIS.

MARGARET'S MOTHER WILL BE CALLING LATER TO SCHEDULE A VISIT. OBLIGE HER.

Bloop Bloop

skriiii

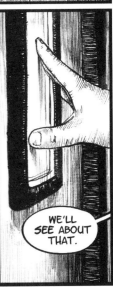

WE'LL SEE ABOUT THAT.

hEY!

hey Dr. oJay!

dR. oJay!! hey!

hey! Dr. oJay!!

wheww!

aRe WE glad to have found you!!

ROMULUS? WHAT ARE YOU --

raymOnd.

squeek

squeek

PARDON?

tHis one is Raymond.

RAYMOND. RIGHT. SORRY.

NO ONE'S SUPPOSED TO LEAVE THEIR ROOM. DIDN'T YOU HEAR?

yES. we knOw. yes. because Of the dead Barry wInslow...

...and the fInGer. yes.

HOW'D YOU HEAR ABOUT THAT?

WHO TOLD YOU ABOUT THE FINGER?

I cannot say, nO.

but we... yes. We were told you knew. That you weRe awake, nOw.

WE FOUND THIS INDEX FINGER UNDER THE SMALL INTESTINE.

CONTRARY TO RUMOR, IT DID *NOT* GET THERE NATURALLY.

DREADFUL.

Bloop

LOVELY. THEN HOW *DID* IT GET THERE?

THERE WAS A SMALL INCISION I MISTOOK FOR A *TATTOO* NEAR THE AREA.

IT WAS EXTREMELY PRECISE.

VAIT. DEN DIS IS A MURDER, CERTAINLY NOW YES?

WHO *KNOWS*, KIPLING? WOULD YOU LIKE SOME TIME *ALONE* WITH THE EVIDENCE?

... YOU KNOW, *MAN* TO *FINGER*.

STRAUSS YOU ARE LIKE THE *CHILD*.

ISS TODAY DRESS-UP PARTY DAY *AGAIN*? TOO BAD I FORGOT *MY* COSTUME.

KIPLING, YOU *SCAB*, YOUR TIME WILL COME, MARK MY WORDS.

MAYBE *YOU* ARE THIS KILLER, MR. SUPERHERO PANTS, *HMMM*?

ENOUGH. LET'S KEEP THE FEUD ON THE FARM, SHALL WE?

FOR ONCE I AGREE.

NOW. ANYONE HAVE SOMETHING *HELPFUL* TO OFFER TO THIS MESS?

HAVE YOU CONSIDERED THE POSSIBILITY THAT JULIUS MAY BE CONNECTED WITH THE SITUATION?

THE TWINS DID SPOT HIM ON THEIR FLOOR...

IF THE TIMING'S RIGHT, THAT MAY BE SIGNIFICANT.

44

ANOTHER THING...

... THE SYMBOL ON BARRY'S HIP LOOKED FAMILIAR, SO I DUG AROUND IN THE ARCHIVES THIS MORNING.

I FOUND THE EXACT SAME SYMBOL ON SEVERAL DOCUMENTS FROM A GROUP WHO USED TO MEET HERE CALLED *"THE TILLARY SOCIETY"*.

THIS SPECIFIC SYMBOL WAS OF PARTICULAR INTEREST TO THE GROUP.

BUT VAT DOES IT HAFF TO DO VIT POOR BARRY'S *DEATH?*

BEAR WITH ME, HERE...

... THE *WEIRD* BIT WAS THAT ALL THESE FILES WERE LAID OUT AS IF THEY WERE *INTENDED* TO BE FOUND.

BUT IT DIDN'T LOOK LIKE ANYONE HAD BEEN DOWN THERE FOR *YEARS*...

WHAT WERE THE RECORDS ABOUT?

GEOMANCY AND URBAN PLANNING.

OKAY... THAT *IS* WEIRD.

WAIT... WASN'T BARRY FOUND NEAR THE ARCHIVES?

YEAH, BUT HE WASN'T MUCH FOR READING. MORE OF A *TV GUY.*

WHY ARE WE EVEN *TRYING* TO FIGURE THIS OUT? ISN'T THIS SOMETHING FOR THE *POLICE?*

APPARENTLY *NOT.* ORDERS FROM THE BOARD.

THEY'RE WORRIED THE PUBLIC MIGHT *CONNECT* THIS WITH COMMISIONER SPARK'S RECENT *ARRIVAL* HERE.

HOW DO WE KNOW THEY'RE *NOT* CONNECTED?

SUSAN'S *RIGHT.*

45

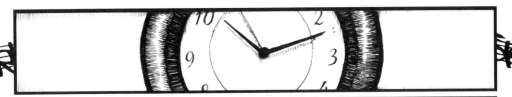

THE HELL IS GOING ON HERE?

DAVID!

WHAT? OH SUSAN.

I HOPE I'M NOT DISTURBING YOU.

klik

NO ... I WAS HEADED TO THE GALLEY.

IT SOUNDED LIKE YOU WERE BUTCHERING PIGS BACK HERE.

AH ... YES, THE MUSIC.

"I'VE SYNCHRONIZED THE DNA SEQUENCE OF A SALT WATER PIKE AND ASSIGNED IT NOTES ON A TEN OCTAVE SCALE."

THIS IS WHAT "FISH" SOUNDS LIKE!

IT'S SPLENDID, DON'T YOU THINK?

UMM...

... I'M NOT SURE IF SPLENDID IS THE WORD I'D USE.

47

AAHH...

LIKE MANY THINGS, AN *ACQUIRED* TASTE.

HAS ANYONE EVER TOLD YOU WHAT HAPPENED THE LAST TIME JULIUS AWOKE?

LOUIS ALWAYS *CHANGES* THE SUBJECT WHEN I BRING IT UP.

YES, I KNOW... TO HIS GREAT PERIL, DR. GENARO LIVES IN DENIAL.

"WE HAD NEVER ENCOUNTERED A CASE LIKE JULIUS' BEFORE."

"GEORGE VLADEK WAS CHIEF THEN. HE HAD NEVER ACCEPTED JULIUS' CATATONIA AS PHYSIOLOGICAL."

"HE WAS CONVINCED JULIUS WAS MERELY *STUDYING* US, INSTEAD. *WAITING* FOR SOMETHING."

"UNFORTUNATELY FOR US BOTH HE WAS *RIGHT*."

"WE THOUGHT WE WERE IN CHARGE. WE THOUGHT WE HAD CONTROL..."

... BUT INSTEAD, IT WAS *JULIUS* WHO HAD SET THE TRAP.

IT... IT ALL HAPPENED SO *FAST*. LIKE A RATTLESNAKE STRIKING.

IT WAS AS IF DR. VLADEK HAD BEEN THROWN HEADLONG DOWN AN IMPOSSIBLY LONG CORRIDOR.

"IT WAS THE LAST THING I EVER SAW. THEN JULIUS TOOK MY *EYES*."

THEY *DID* SOMETHING TO US, SUSAN. WE HAVE *BEEN* HERE BEFORE.

WE JUST DON'T SEEM TO REMEMBER.

WAIT... YOU *LOST* ME.

YOU CAN'T *UNDERSTAND*... *I'M* THE ONLY PASSENGER ON A PLANE THAT KNOWS IT'S ABOUT TO *CRASH*.

SO *MAKE* ME UNDERSTAND, DAVID.

BUT THAT'S THE JOKE OF MEMORY. YOU'RE GOING TO HAVE TO COME TO IT *YOURSELF*.

I'M AFRAID I DO KNOW THIS MUCH: AT THE END, IT WILL ALL COME DOWN TO YOU AND YOU ALONE.

OKAY, NOW YOU'RE STARTING TO FREAK ME OUT.

I PROMISE I WILL DO EVERYTHING I CAN TO HELP YOU, MY DEAR.

YOU SHOULD GO.

BUT DAVID...

DON'T WORRY...

...WE *WILL* TALK ABOUT THIS AGAIN BEFORE IT'S ALL OVER.

AND SUSAN...

...I'M SO VERY SORRY FOR WHAT'S COMING NEXT.

THREE DAYS LEFT

GOODBYE.

MARGARET?

SQUEEK
SQUEI

EASY...

NO! BACK! BACK!

NO, THIS WAY!

SQUEEK S

SKREE
EEC

WAIT!

THUD

TAK

THAT'S GREAT. THAT'S JUST PEACHY.

NOW YOU'VE BROKEN THE OTHER WHEEL.

WHAT? I BROKE THE WHEEL?

LIFT AND PUSH WAS YOUR IDEA, STRAUSS!

WELL, AT LEAST SHE DIDN'T FALL ONTO THE FLOOR AGAIN.

SQUEEK SQUEEK

HEY LOUIS, HAVE YOU TOLD SUSAN YET?

HAVEN'T HAD A CHANCE YET. WHY?

HERE COMES YOUR CHANCE RIGHT NOW.

CHRIST...

... EVERYONE JUST KEEP QUIET. THIS HAS TO BE HANDLED VERY DELICATELY.

57

GOOD MORNING, ALICE.

I'D LIKE TO APOLOGIZE FOR THE RATHER *LATE* SESSION TODAY...

WE'VE HAD SOME, UH, WELL ...

... RECENT *TRAGEDIES* THAT HAVE CAUSED A BIT OF--

I *KNOW*, DOCTOR.

THE LITTLE BOY TOLD ME.

UH... WHAT?

WHAT... DID YOU JUST SAY?

THE LITTLE BOY WITH THE PROSTHETIC ARMS. HE'S BEEN COMING BY *EVERY* NIGHT SINCE I CAME HERE.

JULIUS? YOU MEAN JULIUS HAS BEEN *VISITNG* YOU AT NIGHT?

DO... YOU KNOW *WHY?*

... NO. I THOUGHT YOU MIGHT.

ME? WHY?

COME ON, DOCTOR. I'M NOT STUPID.

ISN'T HE PART OF THE THERAPY?

YOU KNOW... SOFTEN UP THE CHILD KILLER WITH A CUTE LITTLE BOY TO REMIND ME OF MY DEAD SON, ETC?

WOW, THAT'S BITTER.

ACTUALLY, I'M NOT HERE TO TREAT YOU AT ALL. I'M JUST SUPPOSED TO EVALUATE YOUR ABILITY TO STAND TRIAL.

AH. AND WHAT HAVE YOU DECIDED THEN?

I HAVEN'T YET.

SO ... WHAT ARE YOU WAITING FOR?

I'M ALERT, SANE, EVEN BITTER. SO WHAT'S THE HOLD UP?

SO YOU THINK YOU'RE GUILTY.

I KNOW I AM.

BURNED THE HOUSE, KILLED THE FAMILY.

GUILTY AS CHARGED.

YOU SEEM EAGER FOR PUNISHMENT.

... FUCK OFF.

60

TWO DAYS LEFT

IT'S BAD, RIGHT? YOU THINK IT LOOKS BAD. BE HONEST.

AND THE *NAILS*, LOUIS...

... DON'T FORGET THE *NAILS*.

OKAY... IT LOOKS LIKE SOMEONE GLUED A *TOMATO* TO YOUR FACE.

I TAKE IT BACK. *LIE* TO ME.

LOOKS LIKE *YOU* FOUND THE BEAUTY PARLOR. NEW HAIR, YES?

YES, YES. VERY "ELVIRA".

THE BOARD JUST CONTACTED ME. THEY'RE SENDING OUT A SPECIAL *LIAISON*, TO "HANDLE" THE RECENT MURDERS.

AND THE *POLICE* ARE...

NOT TO BE CONTACTED.

I THINK BARNES IS *RIGHT* ABOUT A COVER-UP. BETWEEN *THIS* AND WATCHING OVER SUSAN'S *KIDS*...

WELL MAYBE YOU SHOULD *CALL* HER THEN. MAKE *PEACE*.

I DON'T KNOW *WHAT'S* GOING ON BETWEEN YOU TWO, BUT I'M *SURE* IT'S NOT ALL HER FAULT.

I SEE YOU FOUND HIS *BEE-BOY* COSTUME.

YEAH... IT'S THE ONLY THING THAT STOPPED HIM *SCREAMING*.

HOW'S IT *GOING*, NICKY?

zzZZRrrt

HIDING FROM
ME WON'T DO YOU
ANY GOOD, YOU
KNOW.

69

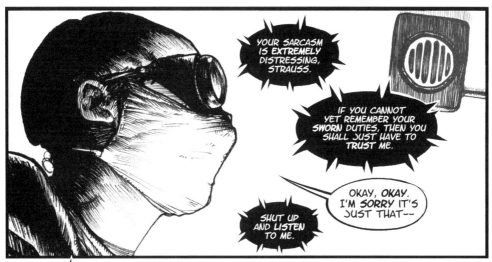

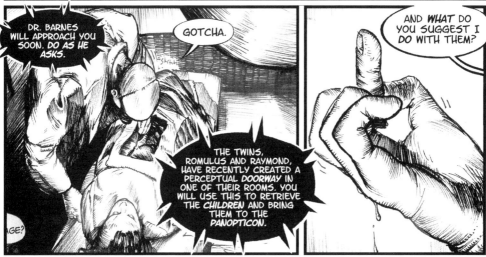

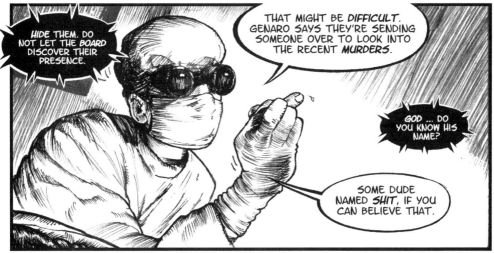

71

IT'S SJIT, ACTUALLY. DR. EINER SJIT.

THIS IS VERY, VERY BAD.

SO ... WHAT DO WE DO?

DR. VLADEK? HEY, WHAT SHOULD WE DO? HELLO? ARE YOU STILL THERE?

... I WAS THINKING.

YOU'LL HAVE TO PROCEED ANYWAY. FOLLOW BARNES, BUT TELL NO ONE WHAT YOU'RE DOING.

BE CAREFUL, STRAUSS. DR. SJIT IS A VERY DANGEROUS MAN.

IF BARNES SURVIVES HIS AWAKENING TONIGHT, HE MAY BE ABLE TO HELP YOU.

IF I CAN I'LL TRY AND CONTACT YOU AGAIN.

WAIT, BUT WHAT DO I DO IF THE WHOLE MAGIC DOOR BIT DOESN'T, YOU KNOW, WORK?

DR. VLADEK? GEORGE?

SKRRRT

SKRT -ID YOU JUST SKRRT CALL ME GEORGE?

OH, PAMELA HEY... UH I DUNNO. I GUESS THE INTERCOM IS DOING ITS THING AGAIN.

I GUESS WE NEED TO GET IT FIXED.

NO SKRRT KIDDING.

SKRRRTCH

HEY, WASN'T DR. AUGET SUPPOSED TO HELP YOU SKRT WITH MARGARET'S AUTOPSY?

NEVER SHOWED UP, I GUESS.

HEY, PAMELA, COULD YOU TURN DOWN THE HEAT A LITTLE?

IT'S AS HOT AS TEXAS DOWN HERE.

THERE'S NO USE IN TRYING, STRAUSS.

NEVER *COULD* SNEAK UP ON YOU, BARNES.

LISTEN ... UH, I WANTED TO ... *TALK* TO YOU.

FIRST, DO ME A SMALL *FAVOR*...

... PLEASE TELL ME WHAT'S DEPICTED IN THIS PAINTING.

WELL, IT'S OF US, DAVID.

IT'S A PAINTING OF *US*, LOOKING AT A PAINTING OF *US*.

IT'S KIND OF WHAT I WANTED TO *TALK* TO YOU ABOUT.

MAN, THESE THINGS REALLY GIVE ME THE *WILLIES*.

IT'S LIKE SEEING YOURSELF ON *TV* ... LIKE WE'RE IN SOME KIND OF WEIRDO *STORY*.

HMPH.

LET'S GO. THERE'S SOMETHING *ELSE* I WANT TO SHOW YOU.

HEY...

DO YOU THINK IT'S POSSIBLE TO PAINT SOMETHING SO *REALISTIC* YOU CAN ACTUALLY WALK *INTO* IT?

74

PERSONALLY SPEAKING, NO. I DON'T THINK SO.

ALTHOUGH ROMULUS AND RAYMOND SEEM TO BELIEVE *OTHERWISE*.

EVEN THE MOST *CONVINCING* OF PHOTOGRAPHS BENDS YOUR NOSE WHEN PRESSED AGAINST IT.

ULP... OKAY. PLEASE GO ON ...

YEARS AGO THEY *HAD* PAINTED A *VERY* REALISTIC MURAL OF CENTRAL PARK AND SHORTLY AFTER ESCAPED.

THEY WERE *EVEN* SAID TO HAVE BEEN APPREHENDED NEAR BETHESDA FOUNTAIN.

REALLY?

VLADEK HAD THE MURAL PAINTED OVER AND THE TWINS *SWORE* AGAINST EVER REPEATING THE SIN.

NO, OF *COURSE* NOT.

VLADEK WAS A *MERRY-ANDREW* AND OFTEN PLAYED SUCH PRANKS ON THE STAFF.

HAVE YOU, UH, *SPOKEN* WITH DR. VLADEK ... *RECENTLY?*

DON'T BE SILLY. GEORGE VLADEK IS *DEAD*, EMIL.

NOW. THE LITTLE BEASTS HAVE BEEN *DOING* SOMETHING IN HERE FOR SOME TIME NOW.

I NEED YOU TO *TELL* ME WHAT IT IS, PLEASE.

UHH... DO I HAVE TO GO *FIRST?*

FOR *CHRISSAKES*, STRAUSS.

NOW, *WHAT* DO YOU *SEE?*

IT'S... IT'S A *MURAL*, I GUESS. IT COVERS ALL THE WALLS AND CEILINGS.

IT'S LIKE NOTHING I'VE EVER *SEEN* BEFORE.

HOLY *SHIT*, THERE'S EVEN A *DRAFT!* DO YOU FEEL IT?

... YES.

SNIFF

SNIFF

PHEW... PISS AND MADNESS.

if only...

HA!!

HEH ... SORRY ABOUT THAT...

... ROACH.

SO DOCTOR, WHAT'S TODAY'S PUNISHMENT?

HEH ...

... WELL I'VE BEEN DOING A LOT OF RESEARCH INTO YOUR CASE.

IS THIS IN ANY WAY GOING TO EXPLAIN THE NEW HAIRDO?

HEH...

IT ENDS HERE.

AFTER ALL I'VE BEEN THROUGH ...

... AFTER ALL I HAVE NOW SUFFERED.

SUCH *STAGNATION*.

ALL THESE YEARS I HAVE WAITED FOR IT TO COME.

AND NOW IT'S HAPPENING, AND I AM SHUT AWAY FROM IT.

MY GREAT FORGOTTEN TASK, *LOST* TO ME NOW.

WELL, NO MORE.

CLICK

SJIT-1

IF THE ANSWERS REFUSE TO COME TO *ME*...

... THEN *I* SHALL RACE TOWARDS *THEM*.

JESUS!

DON'T YOU KNOW IT'S *RUDE* TO SNEAK UP ON PEOPLE?

YOU'D *RUN* IF YOU SAW ME COMING.

AND YOU'D BE *WISE* TO.

AND *YOU* ARE ...?

DR. EINER SJIT. I'M FROM THE *BOARD*.

I'M *SORRY* THERE WAS NO ONE TO MEET YOU AT THE *DOOR*.

WE DIDN'T EXPECT YOU UNTIL SOMETIME *TOMORROW*.

WELL... CHRISTMAS CAME *EARLY* FOR YOU THIS YEAR THEN, *DIDN'T* IT?

LET'S JUST GET RIGHT TO IT, SHALL WE?

WE'VE BEEN *OBSERVING* THE SITUATION HERE FOR SOME TIME NOW, GENARO.

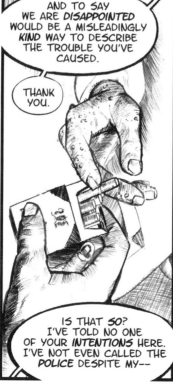

AND TO SAY WE ARE *DISAPPOINTED* WOULD BE A MISLEADINGLY *KIND* WAY TO DESCRIBE THE TROUBLE YOU'VE CAUSED.

THANK YOU.

IS THAT *SO*? I'VE TOLD NO ONE OF YOUR *INTENTIONS* HERE. I'VE NOT EVEN CALLED THE *POLICE* DESPITE MY--

THANK *GOD* AT LEAST FOR *THAT* SMALL MIRACLE.

IT'S A MENINGEAL *ECZEMA*.

EXCUSE ME?

IN VICTORIAN TIMES IT WAS *KINDLY* REFERRED TO AS "CHICKEN SKIN".

IT COVERS A GOOD PORTION OF MY BODY, *NOT* EXCLUDING MY GENITALS.

... IT DISGUSTS YOU

BUT I NEVER SAID--

NOR WOULD YOU HAVE.

I'VE BEEN POKING AROUND YOUR LITTLE HOSPITAL FOR THREE DAYS NOW ...

... AND I MUST SAY, YOU RUN A SLOPPY SHIP, SIR.

YOU'VE GOT PATIENTS KILLING PATIENTS, AND SECURITY'S A JOKE. EVEN UNDER LOCKDOWN I'VE MANAGED TO EASILY COME AND GO AT MY LEISURE.

YOUR INCOMPETENCE IS STUNNING, REALLY.

YOU EVEN LEAVE HIGHLY RESTRICTED DOCUMENTS JUST LYING ABOUT FOR ANYONE TO PICK UP.

WAIT. YOU'VE BEEN HERE HOW LONG?

DO YOU EVEN KNOW WHAT THIS IS?

DR. AUGET DISCOVERED IT ON ONE OF THE VICTIMS.

APPARENTLY IT'S CONNECTED WITH SOME OLD SECRET SOCIETY CALLED--

YOU'RE JUST LIKE A MONKEY.

HA HAHH...

... LIKE A MONKEY HOLDING A CELLPHONE YOU HAVE NO IDEA WHAT'S SITTING RIGHT IN FRONT OF YOU.

HA HA HA HAH HEH AH HA!!

AH HAH HAH HAH HA HAH!!

THE BRIEF MOMENTS OF HESITATION SHATTER WITH EVERY BLARING HORN...

THE DEAD SKIN OF MY LIFE, FALLING AWAY.

MY TEETH CLENCH INTO A FEROCIOUS SMILE.

HMPH...

...

I GUESS IT'S JUST THE "WIND".

SURELY IT'S NOT MY JUVENILE BOYFRIEND TRYING TO GIVE HIS SWEET AND BEAUTIFUL GIRL A SPOOK.

FOR SAID BOYFRIEND MAY FIND HIMSELF IN A GREAT DEAL OF PAIN IF HE TRIED IT.

EVERYTHING DRIFTS INTO FOCUS.

ALL THAT I SOUGHT IS BEFORE ME NOW.

IT IS IN THIS FELLOWSHIP OF NONE THAT I RECALL THE FORGOTTEN.

STRAUSS, DON'T *MAKE* ME--

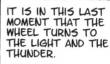

IT IS IN THIS LAST MOMENT THAT THE WHEEL TURNS TO THE LIGHT AND THE THUNDER.

OH! SORRY. I THOUGHT YOU WERE SOMEONE ELSE.

HONK! HONK!

HONK!

AND I LIVE MY LIFE'S PROMISE, WEIGHTLESS OF GRAVITY.

YOU MUST BE THAT GUY THE *BOARD* SENT...

... DR. *SJIT*, RIGHT?

NEVER TO LEAVE THIS WORLD WITH A WHIMPER ...

HONK HON

NO NOT SHIT.

... BUT A *BANG*.

PAMELA?

YOU STILL *DOWN* HERE?

IF WE DON'T GET *GOING*, WE'RE GOING TO MISS THE KILLER, YOU KNOW.

I KNOW HOW YOU *HATE* MISSING THE *PREVIEWS*.

HELLO?

PAMELA?

ONE DAY LEFT

once upon a time there were two children, a boy and a girl, sitting near a stream by a large round castle.

behind them, standing on the barrow, were six very brave warriors each holding the standard of their respective houses.

it was late in the day and the sun had begun to set behind the six brave warriors.

as the two children looked out upon the water rushing by them, the girl, who was older, turned to her brother and spoke.

'brother,' spoke the girl, 'the brave warriors are very afraid.

'they say a storm is coming, and wish to take shelter in the castle until it is safe.'

'they may take refuge in the castle if they wish,' said the boy, 'but it will provide no shelter from the storm that is coming.'

the younger brother turned to his sister slowly, and whispered so that only she could hear his words.

BANG.

98

"IN 1912, A SUDDEN OUTBREAK OF *TUBERCULOSIS* FORCED CITY HEALTH OFFICIALS TO QUARANTINE A *THIRTY-EIGHT* BLOCK RADIUS OF NORTHERN BROOKLYN.

"CONTROL OF THE QUARANTINE AREA FELL UNDER THE JURISDICTION OF THE BENTHAM PANOPTICON, AND ITS CHIEF, DR. ADDISON BONTICOU.

"FOR *TWELVE* WEEKS BENTHAM HOSPITAL WAS IN *TOTAL* CONTROL OF ONE OF THE MOST DENSELY POPULATED REGIONS OF THE CITY.

"DR. BONTICOU BEGAN TO EXERCISE HIS CONTROL IMMEDIATELY.

"*EVERY* CHILD UNDER AGE TEN WAS TO REPORT TO THE HOSPITAL FOR *PREVENTATIVE TREATMENT* AGAINST THE PLAGUE.

"BONTICOU USED AN AGGRESSIVE PHLEBOTOMY TECHNIQUE AS THE *SOLE* METHOD TO DISPATCH THE EPIDEMIC.

"OVER *ONE HUNDRED* CHILDREN WERE DRAINED OF NEARLY *ALL* OF THEIR BLOOD.

"FEW SURVIVED. AN *ENTIRE* GENERATION HAD BEEN LOST IN JUST A *FEW* DAYS, BUT THE PLAGUE ENDED AS SUDDENLY AS IT HAD BEGUN.

"BONTICOU WAS LAUDED AS A PUBLIC *HERO*."

"IT WASN'T UNTIL *1977* THAT THE TRUTH BEHIND THE OUTBREAK CAME TO LIGHT.

"DR. VLADEK HAD FOUND A SECRET ACCOUNT BY DR. BONTICOU'S WIFE OF THE WHOLE AFFAIR IN DETAIL.

"SHE RECORDED THAT *ALL* THE PHLEBOTOMIZED CHILDREN WERE REINFUSED WITH AN UNKNOWN SUBSTANCE.

"MOREOVER, *NONE* HAD DIED AS REPORTED BY THE NASCENT HEALTH DEPARTMENT.

"VLADEK SHOWED THE DOCUMENTS *ONLY* TO A FEW OTHERS AT THE TIME: DR. BARNES, HIS MENTOR, DR. HELLER, AND A YOUNG INTERN NAMED *LOUIS GENARO.*

"APPARENTLY BONTICOU AND *EVERY* SUCCEEDING CHIEF OF STAFF WERE MEMBERS OF AN ANCIENT SECRET ORDER KNOWN AS *THE TILLARY SOCIETY.*

"*OUTLAWED* BY WILLIAM III OF ENGLAND FOR EXPERIMENTS ON *CHILDREN,* THE SOCIETY RELOCATED HERE."

"IN 1878, THEY TOOK OVER THE OPERATION OF *THIS* HOSPITAL.

"FOR YEARS THEY USED BENTHAM TO FURTHER THEIR AIMS, CULMINATING IN THE FALSE PLAGUE OF 1912.

"BUT WHAT WAS THE RESULT OF BONTICOU'S EXPERIMENTS?

"AND WHAT HAPPENED TO THE CHILDREN WHO HAD SURVIVED IT?"

JULIUS
195?-196?

SO...

DO *YOU* KNOW ALICE?

103

AND WHY NOT?

I SAW THAT SNEER OF JUDGEMENT JUST NOW.

YOU JUST DON'T SEEM AS UPSET ABOUT YOUR CHIL—

FUCK YOU, ALL RIGHT! FUCK YOU!!!

I CRY FOR THEM EVERY DAMN DAY.

YOU CAN'T KNOW WHAT IT'S LIKE BEING RAISED BY THAT CULT.

YOU THINK I DIDN'T WANT TO GET THEM OUT OF THERE?

FOR ALL THE THINGS THEY DID TO THEM...

...ALL THAT HE DID TO THEM.

WHO, ALICE?

THE HELL DO YOU CARE ANYWAY?

GO FIND SOME OTHER STAR CRIMINAL TO LAUNCH YOUR PRECIOUS FUCKING CAREER, OKAY?

DAMMIT, WOMAN! I'M TRYING TO *SAVE* YOU, FOR CHIRSSAKES!

I DIDN'T *ASK* YOU TO SAVE ME.

YOU NEVER *NEEDED* TO.

FUCK THAT *SUPERMAN* CRAP.

GIVEN WHAT'S *COMING*, YOU SHOULD WORRY ABOUT SAVING *YOURSELF*.

YOU KNOW THEY'VE *SENT* SOMEONE FOR YOU?!

HE'S GOING TO TAKE YOU *BACK* AND LOCK YOU AWAY IN SOME DAMNED *DUNGEON* FOR THE REST OF YOUR LIFE!!

GODDAMMIT! I DIDN'T EVEN *WANT* THIS CASE!

YOU DIDN'T KILL YOUR KIDS, AND YOU *FUCKING WELL* KNOW IT!

I MIGHT AS *WELL* HAVE.

I LET MY HUSBAND ABUSE THEM FOR *YEARS*, DOCTOR.

I GOT HIGH *EVERY* NIGHT SO I WOULDN'T FACE WHAT WAS GOING ON IN THE NAME OF THE *DAMN* TILLARY SOCIETY.

JESUS ... *THAT'S* WHY WE FOUND *BARBITURATES* IN YOUR BLOOD.

I *COULD* HAVE STOPPED HIM... I COULD HAVE *LEFT*.

BUT I *DIDN'T* AND NOW THEY'RE *GONE*.

ALICE, YOU HAVE TO *HELP* ME. YOU HAVE TO TELL ME *EVERYTHING* YOU CAN ABOUT THE TILLARYS ...

DOCTOR, I WAS SO DRUGGED OUT I COULDN'T --

... *WHAT* THEY WANTED WITH THE *CHILDREN*, WHAT IT HAS TO DO WITH *YOU* AND THE *HOUSING AUTHORITY*... *ALL* OF IT.

YOU SAID BEFORE THAT YOU *REMEMBERED* ME FROM THAT NIGHT.

... YES.

I DON'T KNOW *HOW* THAT'S POSSIBLE, BUT I *KNOW* IT'S TRUE.

IF THAT'S *TRUE*...

... THEN *THAT* MEANS YOU'RE ONE OF *THEM*, TOO.

YOU'VE JUST BEEN MADE TO *FORGET*.

BUT...

... I DON'T SEE *HOW* THAT'S POSSIBLE.

I'LL TELL YOU HOW.

I'LL JUST NEED YOU TO DO *ONE* THING FOR ME, DOCTOR ...

... IT'S *HENRY*.

CALL ME HENRY.

106

HEY, DAVID!

DAVID?

AH, SUSAN. BACK IN THE SADDLE, EH? NOT COME TO DELIVER YOUR FAMOUS RIGHT *HOOK*, I HOPE.

GOOD ONE, BARNES. VERY CLEVER.

THE WINDBLOWN HAIR IS A GOOD LOOK FOR YOU.

VERY "ELVES".

OH, MY DEAR, I'VE JUST HAD THE MOST *ORGASMIC* EXPERIENCE!

"IT WAS ALL SO *VERY* THEATRICAL! THE TRAFFIC *FLYING* ABOUT ME LIKE FALL LEAVES, THE *THUNDERING* OF THAT *MOTOR* BETWEEN MY LEGS ...

"GOD WHAT ECSTASY!

"MY *GLORIOUS* SUICIDE!

"AND THEN I *SAW* HIM, SUSAN.

"NOT AS HE WAS, BUT AS WE ARE ALSO TO BECOME, FULL OF *LIGHT* AND *SMOKE* AND *TEXAS!*

"EVEN THE *SCREAMING* TIRES OF THE *TRUCK* BEARING DOWN ON ME COULD *NOT* DISTRACT ME FROM MY *MEA CULPA.*

"I REMEMBER IT *ALL. EVERYTHING* WE WERE TAUGHT TO *FORGET.*"

IT'S ALL SO *CLEAR* TO ME NOW.

HOW COULD WE HAVE *POSSIBLY* FORGOTTEN SOMETHING SO *TERRIBLE* AND *WONDROUS*?

NE QUA QUAM VACCUM...

HANG *ON...*

... WHAT ARE YOU *SAYING*? YOU WERE ON A *MOTORCYCLE*? *HOW*? I MEAN... WELL... WHERE *IS* IT?

DESTROYED BY THE *TRUCK*, I IMAGINE.

IT *WAS* QUITE A BIG *BOOM*, YOU SEE.

SOME FOOL JUST PARKED IT *RIGHT* ON THE SIDEWALK, SO I KNICKED IT!

ARE YOU TOTALLY *DERANGED?!!* *JESUS*, DAVID, YOU HAVEN'T GOT ANY *EYES!!*

ARE YOU SURE YOU DIDN'T SUSTAIN A *HEAD* INJURY?

...

I CAN *FEEL* HIM NOW. OH, MY DEAR, I CAN *HEAR* HIM BREATHING.

TELL ME SUSAN, HAVE YOU EVER FIRED A *HANDGUN* BEFORE?

JUST *TEN* MINUTES IN THE CLINIC. THAT'S ALL I ASK.

WHERE ARE YOU *GOING?*

HEY!

STAFF MEETING DEAR. *CHOP CHOP!*

ALICE GOES ON TO SAY THAT *SIX* OF *US* HERE WERE TRAINED AND THEN MADE TO FORGET IT ALL UNTIL THE TIME OF THE *EQUINOX.*

YES, YES. BUT SOMETHING'S GONE *WRONG.*

IS THERE ANY MENTION OF THE *BLACK EGGS?*

THIS IS *RIDICULOUS.*

I *AGREE* WITH DR. *WHAT'S-HIS-NAME* OVER THERE.

I'D LIKE EVERYONE TO MEET OUR BOARD LIAISON, DR. EINER SJIT.

MY *GOD!*

I AM NOW *OFFICIALLY* OUTRAGED!

YOU PEOPLE ARE *SUPPOSED* TO BE *SCIENTISTS,* FOR CHRISSAKES!

OKAY, SO *ENLIGHTEN* US WITH YOUR GREAT WISDOM, DR ... *SHIT,* IS IT?.

THAT'S *SJIT,* SWEET-CHEEKS. *TRY TO* REMEMBER IT...

... UNLESS OF COURSE YOU'VE BEEN *TRAINED* NOT TO...

I MUST SAY, IF THIS MEETING'S *ANY* INDICATION OF YOUR MEDICAL PROWESS, IT'D BE A *MERCY* TO YOUR PATIENTS TO JUST *SHOOT* THEM.

THAT'S QUITE *ENOUGH,* SJIT. IF YOU HAVE A *POINT* I SUGGEST YOU REMEMBER WHAT IT *IS* AND *MAKE* IT.

OKAY .... LET'S REVIEW THE GROCERY LIST THEN, *SHALL* WE?

PSYCHOPATHIC *CHILD MURDERER* AND *ARSONIST* AS YOUR *SOLE* SOURCE OF INFORMATION? *CHECK.*

UNBALANCED, AND CURIOUSLY *ABSENT* PSYCHIATRIST DESPERATE TO HIDE A *ROMANTIC* INTEREST IN HIS PATIENT WITH A *BATSHIT CRAZY* CONSPIRACY THEORY? *CHECK!*

111

DR. SJIT...

AND LET'S NOT *FORGET* YOUR RESIDENT COSTUMED JUNKIE PATHOLOGIST AND *CRIME-SCENE* BURGLAR, THE SIMPLE, IF NOT CHILDISH, DR. STRAUSS!

AND WHAT *WERE* WE DOING IN BARRY WINSLOW'S OFFICE THE OTHER NIGHT, *HMMM?*

CARE TO HEAR *MY* THEORY ON THE SUBJECT?

UH...

BARRY FOUND OUT YOU *LOST* YOUR MEDICAL LICENSE FOR STEALING PATIENTS' MEDS AND WAS *BLACKMAILING* YOU, WASN'T HE?

YOU SEE AN OPPORTUNITY IN MS. SPARK'S ARRIVAL AND TAKE IT.

TCH...

KILLING A *DOLT* LIKE BARRY WAS EASY, EVEN FOR *YOU.*

OH, BUT LIKE EVERY PAPERBACK CRIME NOVEL *INSISTS,* SOMETHING WENT AWRY...

... AND POOR, SWEET MARGARET WITNESSING YOUR CRIME PRESENTED THE NEED FOR HER DEATH, AS WELL...

... AND WHAT OF DEAR PAMELA? YOU'D EVEN THROW HER TO THE WIND JUST TO MAINTAIN YOUR DELUDED COVER STORY.

YOU'RE *WAY* OUT OF LINE, SJIT. YOU *CANNOT* HONESTLY EXPECT US TO *BELIEVE* THAT--

WELL, THAT'S THE *DIFFERENCE* BETWEEN US, LOUIS.

I *DON'T* EXPECT YOU TO BUY INTO *MY* MADE-UP *BULLSHIT.*

PARTY TIME IS *OVER*, PEOPLE. AS OF NOW, MS. SPARK IS UNDER *MY* CARE.

ANY MORE *RUMORS* ABOUT HER COLLUSION WITH SOME SECRET SOCIETY TO TAKE OVER THE *CITY* PRIOR TO THE *APOCALYPSE* WILL TRIGGER *IMMEDIATE* DISMISSAL.

DO I MAKE MYSELF *CLEAR*, WARRIORS?

THIS WAS ONCE A HOSPITAL OF SOME *BETTER* REPUTATION...

... AND IT *WILL* BE SO AGAIN. AT LEAST FOR THOSE OF YOU WHO WILL STILL BE *WORKING* HERE. *SORRY*, STRAUSS, I'M SURE THE *CIRCUS* IS STILL HIRING.

it is tOo late, then.

nO...

dO not apologize.

no.

114

OVER *HERE*, LOUIS.

... *OKAY*, STRAUSS. WHAT'S THE *BIG SECRET*?

YOU'LL *JUST THINK* I'M *OUT OF MY TREE*.

THAT SHIP SAILED *LONG AGO*, EMIL.

HEH... *LOOK*. ALL THAT STUFF FROM AUGET'S NOTES?

I *KNOW* WHAT DR. *SJIT* SAID AND ALL, BUT, *WELL*...

... I THINK DR. AUGET'S *RIGHT*. I MEAN IT ALL *FITS*, YOU KNOW...

... WITH WHAT DR. *VLADEK* HAS BEEN SAYING.

STRAUSS... DR. VLADEK HAS BEEN *DEAD* FOR *FIFTEEN* YEARS.

YEAH... I *KNOW*. I'M NOT SO SURE THAT'S *TRUE*.

I'VE BEEN *SEEING* HIM. WELL, I ONLY *SAW* HIM ONCE, BUT WE'VE BEEN TALKING... *REGULARLY*.

I GUESS HE'S IN *TEXAS*, AND THE *TILLARY* PEOPLE ARE COMING AFTER HIM. AND THERE WAS A LOT OF TALK ABOUT *CHILDREN* AND--

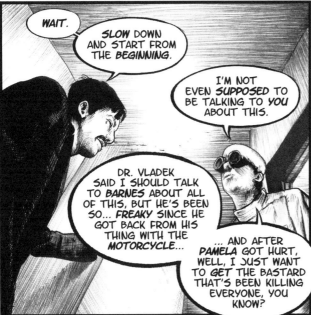

WAIT.

SLOW DOWN AND START FROM THE *BEGINNING*.

I'M NOT EVEN *SUPPOSED* TO BE TALKING TO *YOU* ABOUT THIS.

DR. VLADEK SAID I SHOULD TALK TO *BARNES* ABOUT ALL OF THIS, BUT HE'S BEEN SO... *FREAKY* SINCE HE GOT BACK FROM HIS THING WITH THE *MOTORCYCLE*...

... AND AFTER *PAMELA* GOT HURT, WELL, I JUST WANT TO *GET* THE BASTARD THAT'S BEEN KILLING EVERYONE, YOU KNOW?

I FEEL THE *SAME* WAY, STRAUSS.

JUST START AT THE *BEGINNING*. I WANT YOU TO TELL ME *EVERYTHING*, OKAY?

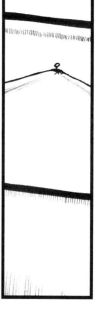

EQUINOX

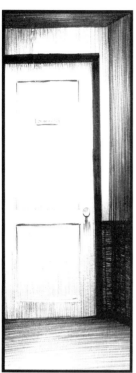

KEF.

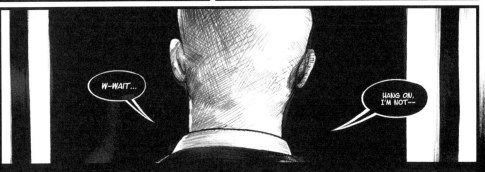

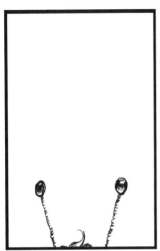

GOOD **MORNING,** SUNSHINE.

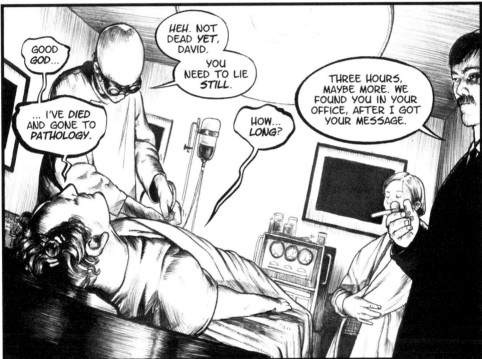

GOOD GOD...

... I'VE *DIED* AND GONE TO *PATHOLOGY.*

HEH. NOT DEAD *YET,* DAVID.

YOU NEED TO LIE *STILL.*

HOW... LONG?

THREE HOURS, MAYBE MORE. WE FOUND YOU IN YOUR OFFICE, AFTER I GOT YOUR MESSAGE.

H-HENRY...

STILL NO SIGN OF HIM. *ALICE SPARK* IS MISSING, TOO.

WE'RE GOING TO STABILIZE YOU, AND THEN EVACUATE THE BUILDING.

N-NO. ...WON'T BE LET YOU...

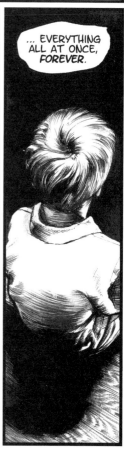

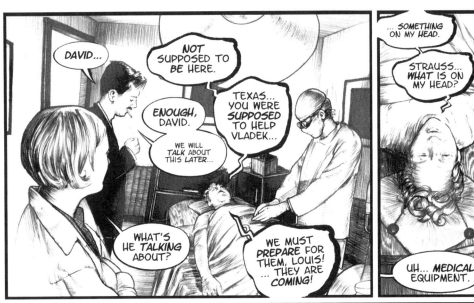

I ONLY WANTED--

THAT WAS THE *MAIN* POWER ...

YEAH...

WE NEED TO GET *EVERYONE* OUT OF HERE.

RIGHT *NOW.*

EQUINOX!

IT'S *BEGUN!* LOUIS, THERE'S NO TIME TO *WASTE!*

DAVID, IF YOU DON'T KEEP *STILL*...

YOU WERE LEFT AWAKE TO AWAKEN THE REST OF US!

FOR GOD'S SAKE, *WHY? WHY* DIDN'T YOU AWAKEN US?!

SUSAN *CAN'T* MEET BONTICOU'S WIFE LIKE *THIS!*

DAMMIT, BARNES...

YOU INCREDIBLE BASTARD.

IT'S *TRUE* ?

IT'S ALL TRUE AND YOU *KNEW* IT ALL THIS TIME?

SUSAN, PLEASE.

YOU DON'T *KNOW* WHAT IT'S BEEN LIKE ...

... WAITING *ALONE* ALL THESE YEARS FOR *SOMETHING* TO HAPPEN.

HELL, I'D WRITTEN IT ALL OFF TO *DELUSION* UNTIL A FEW DAYS AGO WHEN *JULIUS* WOKE UP.

I'M HAVING AS *MUCH* TROUBLE WITH ALL OF THIS AS *YOU* ARE.

I JUST DON'T HAVE THE LUXURY OF SELF-INDUCED *AMNESIA* TO COMFORT ME NOW.

TO BE HONEST, I *ENVY* YOU.

WHAT ARE YOU DOING?

THERE'S NO TIME TO WAKE YOU ALL UP PROPERLY.

GOD, I WISH THERE WAS...

YOU COULD HAVE COME TO ME *EARLIER* ABOUT THIS, LOUIS.

PROBABLY *NOT*...

WOULD YOU HAVE *BELIEVED* ME IF I *HAD*?

TAKE THIS. SET IT TO "13" TO PATCH INTO THE *INTERCOM*.

THE RANGE IS PRETTY CRAPPY, BUT IT SHOULD WORK.

WHAT'S THIS FOR?

YOU'RE GOING TO GET THOSE *FILES* AND ALICE'S AFFIDAVIT FROM MY OFFICE.

AND WHERE ARE *YOU* GOING?

THIS IS ALL *MY* FAULT, SUSAN. I NEED TO TRY AND MAKE IT *RIGHT*.

DON'T WASTE ANY TIME IN THERE, SUSAN.

IN AND *OUT*, OKAY?

IT MAY BE *SOME* TIME BEFORE I *SEE* YOU AGAIN...

... FOLLOW DAVID'S LEAD, AND DO AS HE ASKS.

IF YOU SEE HENRY, *RUN*. HE'S *NOT* THE MAN YOU ONCE KNEW.

134

135

WELL, IT'S ABOUT GODDAMNED *TIME*. YOU KNOW HOW *LONG* I'VE BEEN WAITING HERE IN THE DARK?

THE SHIT'S REALLY *HIT* THE FAN TONIGHT...

I JUST GOT WORD THAT OUR STRIKE AT *VLADEK'S* COMPOUND IN TEXAS GOT *SNUFFED*.

SOMEONE CALLED IN AN ANONYMOUS TIP TO THE ATF *AND* FBI...

... THE WHOLE PLACE IS ON *FIRE*, I HEAR.

SIGH...

THE FACT THAT COMISSIONER SPARK *ISN'T* WITH YOU MEANS WE HAVE TO GO AND *GET* HER NOW I, SUPPOSE...

JESUS! YOU KNOW I NEVER *COULD* FIGURE YOUR LITTLE *CRUSH* ON THAT WOMAN.

DO YOU *REALIZE* HOW MUCH *TROUBLE* PULLING HER FROM THAT *FIRE* HAS CAUSED US?

YOU'D JUST BETTER FUCKING *BE* THERE FOR WHAT NEEDS TO BE DONE *THIS* TIME.

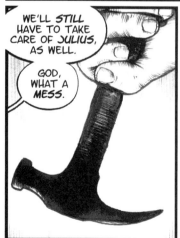

WE'LL *STILL* HAVE TO TAKE CARE OF *JULIUS*, AS WELL.

GOD, WHAT A *MESS*.

ALICE, JULIUS... THAT *WHOLE* CURSED FAMILY LINE WILL FINALLY BE GONE BY *MORNING*.

AT LEAST AFTER ALL THESE *YEARS*, BONTICOU'S MADNESS WILL BE *OVE--*.

LOUIS?

LOUIS, IF YOU CAN *HEAR* ME, I'M HEADING YOUR WAY...

THEY'RE *GONE*, DEAR. BOTH GONE...

SKRRT -GONE *WHERE*, DAVID?

... REMEMBER, WHEN YOU WERE RECOVERING FROM YOUR *FIRST* JAUNT INTO THE NAUGUAL, I *SANG* TO YOU...

"AND ON ♫ THE BANK, OUR BANK, OF THE BLUE, VANISHED WATER..."

Slorp!

♫ "... YOU LIE CRYING IN YOUR BED, HEARING THOSE SMALL, FEARSOME ♫ THRUMPS..."

"... MAY THERE ♫ COME BACK TO YOU A VOICE..."

"... SPECTRAL CALLING YOU, SISTER!" ♫

"SISTER!"

"... FROM ♫ EVERYTHING THAT DIES..."

"AND *THEN* YOU SHALL OPEN THIS BOOK..."

♫ "... EVEN IF IT ♫ IS THE BOOK OF *NIGHTMARES*." ♫

hello...

138

nice lady...

..do you know the way out?

SHIT! SHIT SHITSHIT...

OKAY, DAVID. I *BELIEVE* YOU. TELL ME WHAT I NEED TO DO...

... AND SPEAK UP BECAUSE I'M *RUNNING.*

SKRT –I'LL DO MY BEST...

... THINGS AREN'T *EXACTLY* FOLLOWING THE PLAN, MY DEAR...

SKRT YOU SEE, DEAR, WE ARE IN THE *SHADOW* BENTHAM, NOW. THE HOSPITAL'S *DREAM SELF...*

... YOU ARE THE *HALLERKRIEGER* AND MUST–

FIRE EXIT

A

WAIT–– SHUT UP FOR A SECOND...

DR. *SJIT...*

139

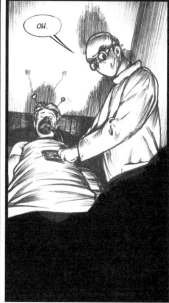

It is precisely this realm of the ineffable that we women share a rare and uncommon predilection over the men who presume to write of it.

And yet, I still would not believe this moment possible...

Such magics are rightfully the provence of fools and small children...

...but still, I waited here for you...

... and here you are.

For six days now they have come like chattel. They believe their children will be innoculated against the disease.

But there is no disease.

The Alienists of this horrid place will grind the bones of their future kin so that they may control the doom they were cursed enough to recognize...

... but they shall not have mine, Hallerkreiger.

My son shall be Caesar over these men of science and maths.

149

OKAY, I'LL ADMIT THAT'S FAIRLY AMAZING, BUT I'VE GOT A *BETTER* IDEA.

-LEASE TE ME ABOUT YC CONTACT WIT BONTICOU'S- *SKRT*

THAT'S GOING TO HAVE TO *WAIT* FOR NOW.

BUT SUSAN, THE SIGNIFICANCE OF WHAT IT MEANS TO FINALLY –

SHUT UP AND *LISTEN* TO ME. YOU ALWAYS SAID THE TWINS WERE LIKE *ONE* PERSON IN TWO BODIES, RIGHT?

SSHHHH, RAYMOND. IT'S OKAY. IT'S GOING TO BE OKAY...

PERHAPS WE CAN USE *RAYMOND* TO FIND *ROMULUS*...

AND IF *HE'S* NEAR HENRY...

... THEN YOU FIND *HENRY* AS WELL. CLEVER GIRL, SUSAN.

... NO JACKET THEN?

BUT WHY WOULD HE HAVE ROMULUS WITH HIM? *SKRRT*

BECAUSE I THINK HE *WANTS* ME TO FIND HIM.

IT'S FAR TOO DANGEROUS MY DEAR...

IF YOU'VE GOT A *BETTER* PLAN, LET'S HEAR IT.

I'M SWITCHING YOU *OFF*, DAVID. CAN'T RUIN THE ELEMENT OF *SURPRISE*.

NO! WAIT YOU CAN'T *SKRT* *CLICK*

150

MAN, OH MAN...

TCH...

I BET YOU WISH YOU HAD YOUR BROTHER'S *POGO-STICK* LEG INSTEAD OF THAT *WHEEL.*

snOrk!

COME ON...

... STAY *CLOSE* AND TRY AND LET ME KNOW WHEN WE'RE NEAR YOUR *BROTHER.*

DROOL, FART, I DON'T REALLY *CARE....* JUST KEEP IT *QUIET.*

... DAVID? WE'RE AT THE TOP OF THE TOWER.

I THINK WE'VE FOUND THEM.

SKRT JUST MAKE SURE THE SAFETY'S OFF, SUSAN.

IS IS THAT WE MUST FULFILL WHAT WE ARE PROMISED...

... OR WHAT WE ARE COMMANDED TO DO?

ALICE?

GO BACK.

... AND I REMEMBER WHO I AM.

I'M AWAKE NOW, SUSAN...

I'M THE VILLAIN.

WHAT THE HELL ARE YOU TALKING ABOUT?

IS THIS IT? IS THIS HOW IT TURNS OUT IN THE END? YOU'RE SICK, HENRY. YOU NEED HELP!

NOW PUT DOWN THE DAMN GUN!

I... IT WASN'T SUPPOSED TO HAPPEN LIKE THIS.

NO SHIT, HENRY.

BACK AWAY FROM ALICE.

WHERE'S ROMULUS?

ROMULUS IS FINE.

kef

JULIUS' BLOOD FLOWS THROUGH HER VEINS.

AND THEN

And i'm not
in the Tree
anymore...

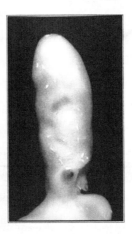

GREG RUTH
(1836-1970)

Odorous and often wet to the touch,
this underwhelming paripatetic scoundrel sits
before you mercifully oblivious, thanks to
a copious supply of medication, to any human
cruelty or recognizeable grace. Before
coming to Bentham, this poor specimen was
forced to reside in an empty avocado crate
for the first decade of his sorry life, scribbling
useless tales of woe and slapstick upon the
exposed, masticated flesh of any unsuspecting
vagabond who dared sleep too closely .

His list of novelties includes four
seperate stories for the Matrix Comics under
Burlyman Entertainment, three for Paradox
Press, two for *The Duplex Planet Illustrated* for
Fantagraphics Books, *Freaks of the Heartland*
and six issues of *Conan* for Dark Horse Comics,
a bit of art for National Geographic Magazine,
and several works on unspeakable joy
for Scholastic Books.

*(Excerpts from this sad fellow's journal and sketchbook
will follow this page.)*

visitation hours can be scheduled by contacting...
www.gregthings.com

October 22 —

Today was oatmeal day. I don't like oatmeal, and no matter how many times I tell the nurses this, it winds up on my plate. I am sure this is on purpose. I shall be strong.

Dr. Auget came in today bald as an egg. I suggested that perhaps his hair was stolen by the nurses who took away my spoon last week. He just smiled.

Something is wrong.

Nicky says nice Dr. Susan was sent home for hitting Dr. Genaro in the face. Maybe he tried to take away her spoon too.

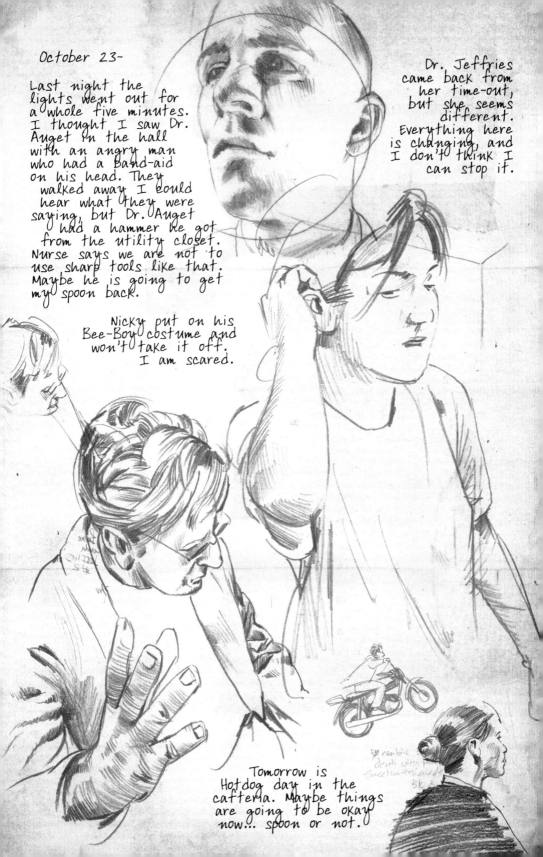

October 23-

Last night the lights went out for a whole five minutes. I thought I saw Dr. Auget in the hall with an angry man who had a Band-aid on his head. They walked away I could hear what they were saying, but Dr. Auget had a hammer he got from the utility closet. Nurse says we are not to use sharp tools like that. Maybe he is going to get my spoon back.

Nicky put on his Bee-Boy costume and won't take it off. I am scared.

Dr. Jeffries came back from her time-out, but she seems different. Everything here is changing, and I don't think I can stop it.

Tomorrow is Hotdog day in the cafteria. Maybe things are going to be okay now... spoon or not.

BENTHAM INTERNATIONAL HOSPITAL

(PERSONNEL)

Dr. Louis Genaro, *Chief of Staff*

While only recently appointed to the position of Chief, Dr. Genaro has proven his abilities and commitment to the hospital consistently in his 20 years on staff. The Board commends his conduct during the Simms incident and in the dangerous capture of his predecessor. However salt-of-the-earth Genaro may seem he is regarded as being unpredictable, particularly in respect to motivation.

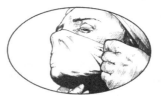

Dr. Henry Auget

Auget is a second generation Criminal Psychologist. Once considered talented in his field, his commitment to his work has been the subject of recent scrutiny. Signs of emotional distraction, ennui, and professional fatigue are evident in his daily interactions and reflected in his repeated attempts to transfer to pathology. All such transfer requests shall be denied with no exceptions on the Board's authority.

Dr. Susan Jeffries

In her short tenure as head of our pediatrics department, Jeffries has exhibited an unparalleled devotion to the children under her care. While this is commendable from a public perspective, her ability to work as a team with other staff is greatly diminished when she perceives any threat to her children. Dr. Jeffries has recently requested historical files related to allegations that this hospital once performed experiments on orphaned children. While her suspicions are, of course, ludicrous and unfounded, she is to be denied any and all access to files extending beyond the last three years.

Dr. David Barnes

Barnes is a valued and knowledgeable senior member of the staff. His unusual approach to medicine is marked by ruthless dissection of the scientific method. Like many others from his generation, he remains a hearty advocate of the studies of altered perception. A regrettable incident fifteen years ago, involving the boy in room 13, resulted in the loss of both of Dr. Barnes' eyes. We believe his scars from that incident run deeper than the physical. He should be watched closely.

Dr. Emil Strauss

Known internally as the staff eccentric, if such a designation is possible regarding a staff as diverse as this one, Strauss is known more for his distinct personality, rather than for anything directly concerning his actual job. Some associates question his professionalism based on his odd preference for wearing full surgical gear at all times. Our personnel director is more concerned about the apparent absence of any medical credentials verifying his doctorate. An investigation of this matter is due.

Pamela Sweetwater

Ms. Sweetwater has served as the hospital's secretary of admissions for nearly 10 years and is known for her direct and forthright manner. She is known for her smiling face and hearty laugh, which are often directed at whomever she is engaging at the moment. A suspected intimate relationship between Strauss and Ms. Sweetwater brings into question her possible role in shielding the uncertain status of Strauss' credentials.

Dr. George Vladek

Once head of the hospital's Psychology division, Vladek vanished mysteriously during the same unfortunate incident that resulted in the blinding of Dr. Barnes. Due to the excessive length of time since his disappearance, he is presumed dead. Any information to the contrary should be reported to the department of human resources.

BH

Also from Greg Ruth

Written by **Steve Niles**   Art by **Greg Ruth**

Under the weathered skies of America's heartland, and in the wounded hearts of every family in one tiny rural town, a terrible secret has been kept for too many years. Now, a young boy named Trevor must try to keep his younger brother Will from falling victim to the worst fears of a troubled town that can't begin to understand the tragic secret that binds its families together.